max science primary

Journal 1

DISCOVERING THROUGH ENQUIRY

PAT DOWER

SERIES EDITOR: **BOB KIBBLE**

macmillan education

INTERNATIONAL CURRICULUM

Macmillan Education
4 Crinan Street
London N1 9XW
A division of Springer Nature Limited

Companies and representatives throughout the world

Journal ISBN 978-1-380-02153-3

First published 2019

Original design by EMC Design Ltd and Macmillan Education
Page make-up by Ink Design
Illustrated by Marna Hattingh
Cover design by Sparks Publishing Services Ltd and Macmillan Education
Cover illustration by Star Publishing Pte Ltd and Jorge Santillan c/o Beehive Illustration Agency
Picture research by Susannah Jayes

Printed and bound in India
2023 2022 2021 2020 2019
10 9 8 7 6 5 4 3 2 1

Contents

Introducing the *Max Science* Journal

The ***Max Science primary* Journal** complements the ***Max Science primary*** series by providing a link between learning at school and learning at home. It matches the topics from the course and the Cambridge Primary Science Curriculum framework with a topic-by-topic series of structured activities for learners to complete with an adult.

As a parent or carer, it is sometimes difficult to know what is being taught in school and how your child is really doing in a subject. Do they enjoy it? Do they understand the concepts and the vocabulary? This Journal lets you spend time with your learner at home in a supportive way and find out how they are doing in science.

Introducing the topic

A cartoon image and question introduces every science topic in a fun and engaging way.

1 Ourselves

1.1 The human body

Some things the same, some things different

Humans are not exactly the same as one another either. We have differences that allow us to tell one another apart.

Look at the cartoon.

Both children have a head.

What other things can you see that are the same?

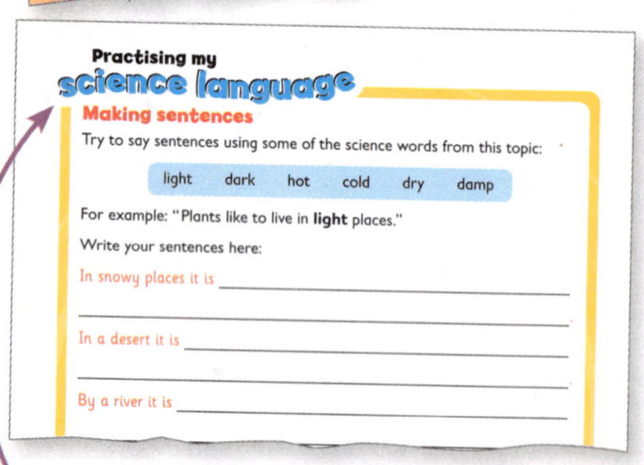
Practising my science language

Making sentences

Try to say sentences using some of the science words from this topic:

light dark hot cold dry damp

For example: "Plants like to live in **light** places."

Write your sentences here:

In snowy places it is ______

In a desert it is ______

By a river it is ______

Practising my science language

This feature provides language practice of key words to improve scientific vocabulary and to make it easier to learn science in English.

Check my science

Each topic allows learners to check their understanding through this activity.

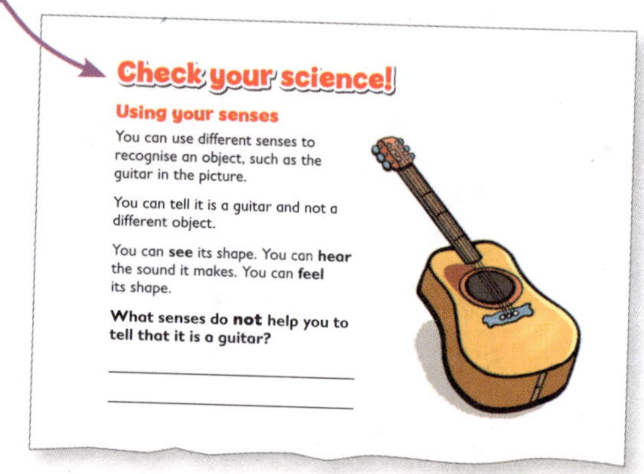
Check your science!

Using your senses

You can use different senses to recognise an object, such as the guitar in the picture.

You can tell it is a guitar and not a different object.

You can **see** its shape. You can **hear** the sound it makes. You can **feel** its shape.

What senses do **not** help you to tell that it is a guitar?

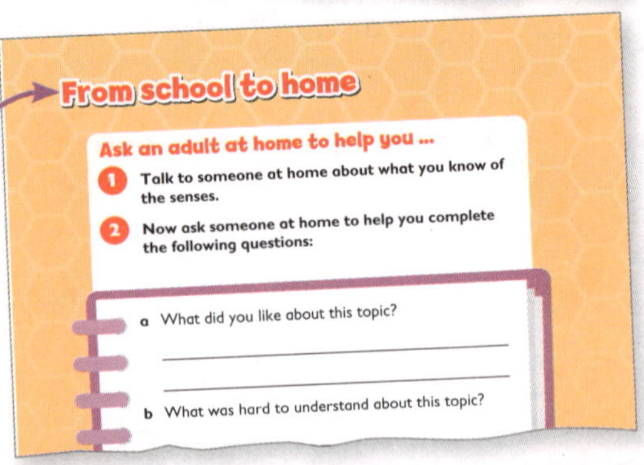
From school to home

Ask an adult at home to help you ...

1 Talk to someone at home about what you know of the senses.

2 Now ask someone at home to help you complete the following questions:

a What did you like about this topic?

b What was hard to understand about this topic?

From school to home

You can work together at home to complete this section at the end of each topic. The Journal can then be taken into school for the teacher to look at and discuss, and acts as a record of the learners' progress.

1 Ourselves

1.1 The human body

Some things the same, some things different

Humans are not exactly the same as one another. We have differences that allow us to tell one another apart.

Look at the cartoon.

Both children have a head.

What other things can you see that are the same?

____

____

____

____

One child is taller than the other.

What other things can you see that are different?

____

____

____

____

Check your science!

Naming parts of the human body

Work with someone at home.

How many parts of the body can you name?

Point to the outline and say the name of each part.

Which of these ones did you get? Tick the boxes.

head	☐	leg	☐	foot	☐
ear	☐	shoulder	☐	hand	☐

Can you name any more parts?

Label them on the outline.

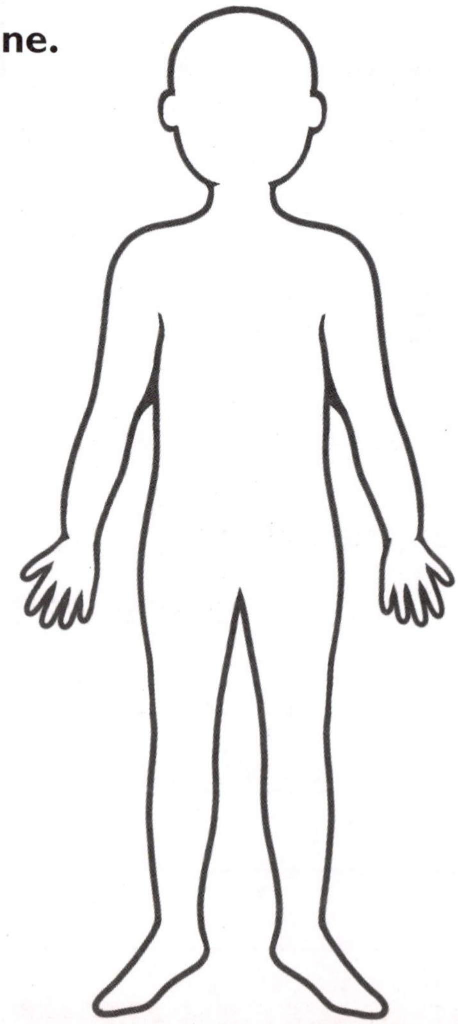

Practising my

science language

Finding words

Look at the word puzzle. Can you find all nine hidden words? There are pictures to help you with six of the words.

An example has been done for you.

r	p	x	q	w	a	k	i	t	k
s	m	q	f	y	v	n	q	g	e
s	**h**	o	u	l	d	e	r	p	a
l	**e**	g	z	v	f	e	h	s	r
c	**a**	o	a	g	k	u	e	b	h
a	**d**	i	f	f	e	r	e	n	t
b	n	h	a	i	r	p	u	b	x
y	i	j	a	d	z	s	a	m	e
b	p	f	o	o	t	h	e	h	r

head ✓

foot 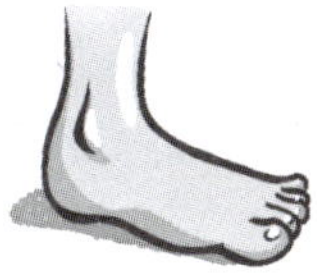

leg 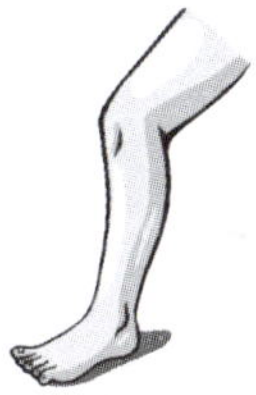

same

different

shoulder 

ear 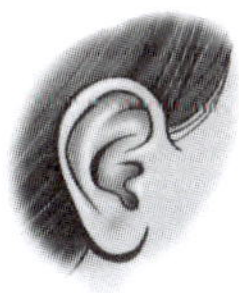

hair 

knee 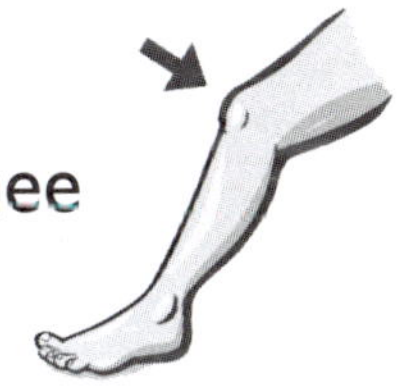

Sentences

Say these sentences to someone at home. Put in your own words to talk about your body. For example: "We both have blue eyes."

"We have some things that are the same."

"We both have ______________________________."

"We are different in some ways."

"I have ______________ but you have ______________."

From school to home

Ask an adult at home to help you ...

1. **Talk to someone at home about what you know of the human body and its parts.**
2. **Now ask someone at home to help you complete the following questions:**

a What did you like about this topic?

____

____

b What was hard to understand about this topic?

____

____

I understand. | I understand a bit. | I need more time to understand this.

3 **Look again at the checklist below. How are you doing now? Circle one face for each statement.**

- I can say how humans are the same.
- I can say how humans can be different.
- I can name parts of the human body.

4 **Ask an adult at home to read and sign this.**

I have checked learning on this topic.

We have shared some understanding at home.

Signed: ______________________

Date: ______________

Teacher comment: ____________________________

____

Date: ______________

1.2 Sensing

Our senses tell us about our surroundings

We have five senses: sight (seeing), hearing, smell, taste and touch (feeling).

Our five senses tell us about our surroundings.

They can tell us about danger close by. They tell us where to find things around us.

Put on a blindfold. Ask someone at home to give you a mystery object.

Feel it. Smell it. Listen to any sounds it makes. Then complete the sentences.

It feels ______________________________.

It smells ______________________________.

Did the object make any sounds? Circle your answer: Yes No

What were the sounds like, if you heard any?

Use the words from the box, or use your own.

loud	soft	high	low	squeaky	scratchy

____

Check your science!

Using your senses

You can use different senses to recognise an object, such as the guitar in the picture.

You can tell it is a guitar and not a different object.

You can **see** its shape. You can **hear** the sound it makes. You can **feel** its shape.

What senses do not help you to tell that it is a guitar?

____

____

Name two senses you could use to tell the banana apart from the apple.

I could use my sense of ________________________

and my sense of ____________________________.

Practising my
science language

Matching

Draw lines to match the words to the pictures.

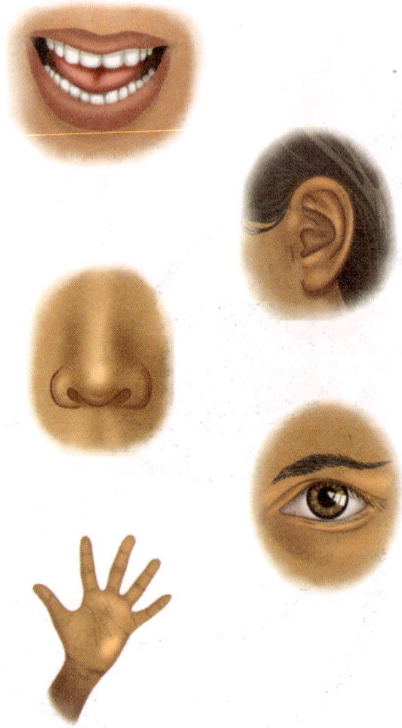

sight

taste

touch

smell

hearing

Missing words

Complete the sentences. Use the words from the box to help you.

smell	touch	sight	hearing	taste

I use my sense of ____________ to see what my dinner looks like.

I use my sense of ____________ to listen to music.

My sense of ____________ tells me that food is cooking in the next room.

I can ____________ a kebab to find out how spicy it is.

My sense of ____________ tells me how soft a towel is.

Say the complete sentences to someone else at home.

From school to home

Ask an adult at home to help you ...

1. Talk to someone at home about what you know of the senses.
2. Now ask someone at home to help you complete the following questions:

a What did you like about this topic?

____

____

b What was hard to understand about this topic?

____

____

I understand. I understand a bit. I need more time to understand this.

3 **Look again at the checklist below. How are you doing now? Circle one face for each statement.**

- I can say what the five senses do.
- I can say what my senses tell me about my surroundings.
- I can say how humans and animals use senses.

4 **Ask an adult at home to read and sign this.**

I have checked learning on this topic.

We have shared some understanding at home.

Signed: ______________________

Date: ______________

Teacher comment: ______________________________

____

Date: ______________

2 What is it made of?

2.1 Exploring materials

Things are made from different materials

A material is what something is made from. Metal, wood and plastic are all types of material.

Material can also mean fabric. The fabrics that clothes are made from, such as cotton and wool, are also materials.

Who is right? Are they both right? Are they both wrong?

Talk about what you think with someone at home.

Underline the correct answer below and complete the sentence.

I think **the boy is right / the girl is right / they are both right / they are both wrong**

because ______________________________.

Check your science!

Describing materials

You can use different words to describe what materials are like.

Look around your house for different materials.

Find materials to describe, using the same word.

Write their names below, like this:

Objects made of **shiny** materials: a metal fork and a gold necklace

Objects made of **soft** materials: ________________ and ________________

Objects made of **hard** materials: ________________ and ________________

Objects made of **rough** materials: ________________ and ________________

Objects made of **smooth** materials: ________________ and ________________

Objects made of **breakable** materials: ________________ and ________________

Think about the material glass. What makes glass a good material for making windows?

____

____

Practising my

science language

Matching

Draw lines to match the words on the left with what they mean. One has been done for you.

hard	You can see through it.
clear	You can change its shape.
smooth	You cannot squash the material.
bendy	You can slide your hand easily over it.

Science words

Write words from this topic that begin with different letters. Tell someone at home what each word means or show them. For example: For glass, you could show someone a glass bottle.

Words that begin with "m": ____________________

Words that begin with "p": ____________________

Words that begin with "s": ____________________

Words that begin with "w": ____________________

Making sentences

Make sentences with these words in them:

soft waterproof wood metal

One has been done for you.

My clothes are made from **soft** materials.

My umbrella is made of a ____________ material.

My chair is made from ____________.

The car is made from ____________.

From school to home

Ask an adult at home to help you ...

1. Talk to someone at home about what you know of exploring materials with your senses, and what different materials are like.

2. Now ask someone at home to help you complete the following questions:

a What did you like about this topic?

____

____

____

b What was hard to understand about this topic?

____

____

____

I understand. | I understand a bit. | I need more time to understand this.

3 **Look again at the checklist below. How are you doing now? Circle one face for each statement.**

- I can say what a material is.
- I can name at least five different materials.
- I can use words to describe different materials.
- I can give examples of what the materials are used for.

4 **Ask an adult at home to read and sign this.**

I have checked learning on this topic.

We have shared some understanding at home.

Signed: ______________________

Date: ______________

Teacher comment: ______________________________

____

Date: ______________

2.2 Understanding materials

What a material is like is important

The properties of a material are what make it good for doing certain jobs. For example, wood is hard and strong, which makes it a good material for a table.

Which material should the people in the picture choose? ____________

Why should they choose this one?

____

____

____

Look at the picture. What has happened?

____

____

Check your science!

Sorting different materials

Think! Why are different materials used for cooking?

Sort the materials by their properties.

Put these materials into the sorting circles:

plastic	metal	glass	wood	pottery

Can you think of any more materials? Add them.

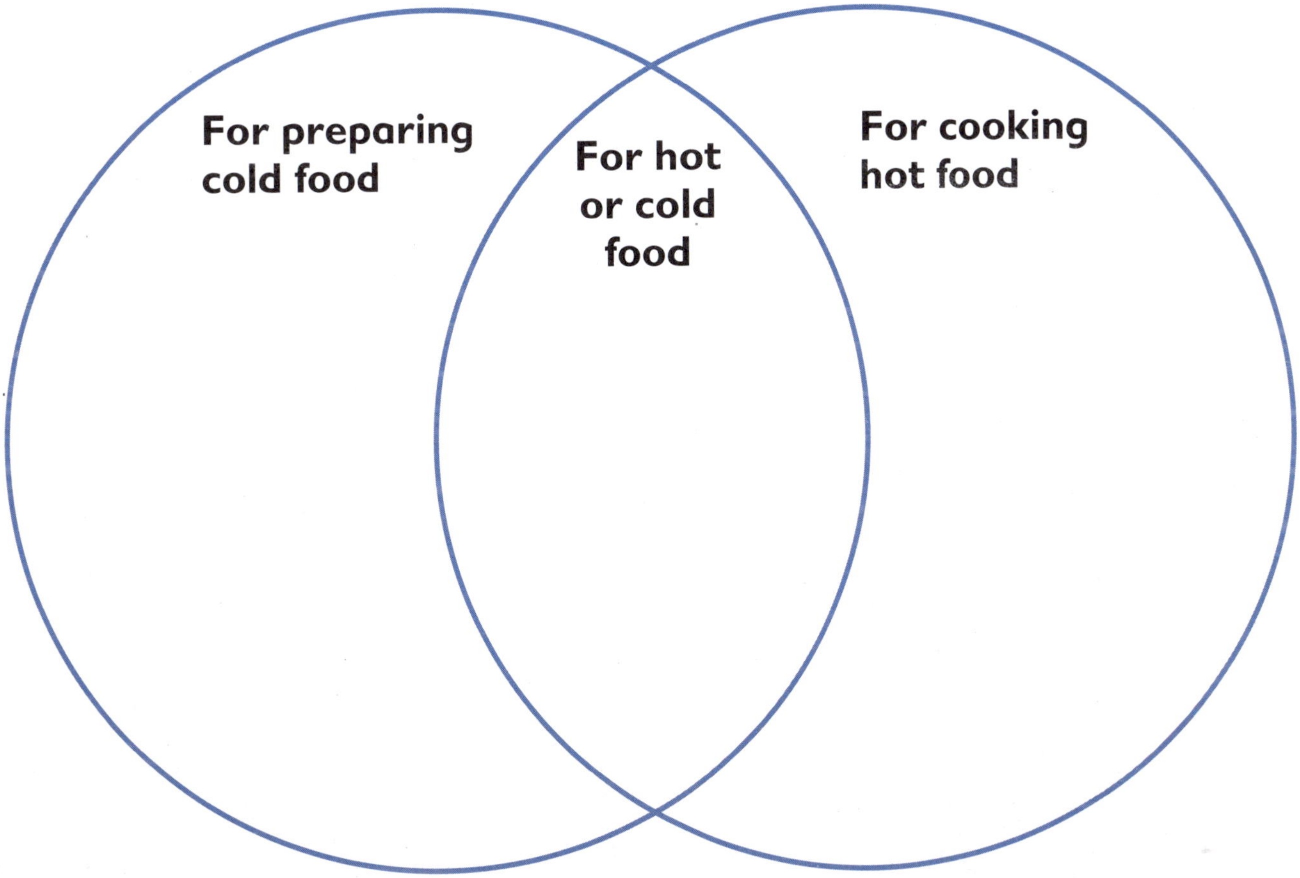

Practising my

science language

Finding words

Find the hidden words in the puzzle to answer the questions.

Draw a ring round the word when you find it.

An example has been done for you.

b	p	z	b	o	d	y	h	s	s	t
h	a	r	d	m	k	m	o	g	o	i
d	i	f	f	e	r	e	n	t	r	e
w	q	p	f	l	v	t	d	q	t	a
m	s	o	f	t	o	a	j	e	y	e
p	d	h	a	q	u	l	y	u	s	m
w	a	t	e	r	p	r	o	o	f	v
o	r	o	p	a	g	n	q	x	i	d
f	y	e	j	m	d	k	q	h	p	r

The material of my clothing feels **soft**. ✔

Stone feels ____________.

The material of a raincoat is ____________.

Coins are made of ____________.

When something is not the same, it is ____________.

When you put things into groups, you ____________ them.

There are three other English words in the puzzle.
Can you find them?

________________ ________________ ________________

Sentences

Is it true? Or is it false? Ask someone at home to tell you.

- Metal is hard. **True** or **false**?
- Glass is soft. **True** or **false**?
- Paper is waterproof. **True** or **false**?
- Foam and cotton are both soft. **True** or **false**?
- Stone is soft and strong. **True** or **false**?
- Many objects are made from plastic. **True** or **false**?

From school to home

Ask an adult at home to help you ...

1. Talk to someone at home about how to sort materials.
2. Now ask someone at home to help you complete the following questions:

a What did you like about this topic?

____

____

____

b What was hard to understand about this topic?

____

____

____

I understand.

I understand a bit.

I need more time to understand this.

3 **Look again at the checklist below. How are you doing now? Circle one face for each statement.**

- I can explain how materials are used for different jobs.
- I can suggest good materials to use for different jobs.
- I can sort materials in different ways.
- I can use the properties of materials to help me sort them.

4 **Ask an adult at home to read and sign this.**

I have checked learning on this topic.

We have shared some understanding at home.

Signed: ______________________

Date: ______________

Teacher comment: ______________________________

____

Date: ______________

3 Living and growing

3.1 Living and non-living

Living things and non-living things are different

Plants and animals are living things. Living things can do things that non-living things cannot do. For example, living things can move on their own. Even the leaves of plants can move.

Living things also take in what they need from around them. All living things take in water.

Non-living things have never been alive. For example, a rock or a piece of metal has never been alive. Dead things were alive once. For example, cut wood was once part of a living tree.

Look at the cartoon.

What do you think?

Is the car moving on its own?

____

____

What makes the car move?

____

____

So, is the car alive?

____

Check your science!

Saying what is alive

Look at the pictures. Tick the things that are living. ✔

Why is it hard sometimes to tell if something is alive?

____

____

Practising my

science language

Sentences

Say these sentences about living things to someone at home. They must answer "yes" or " no".

- I am alive. **Yes** or **no**?
- Trees are non-living things. **Yes** or **no**?
- Plants and animals are living things. **Yes** or **no**?
- A rock is a non-living thing. **Yes** or **no**?
- Living things do not need water. **Yes** or **no**?
- Looking carefully can help you tell if something is alive. **Yes** or **no**?

Mixed-up words

Here are some words from this topic. The letters are all mixed up.

Can you write the words the right way?

For example: vilae can be unmixed as alive.

For each word, one letter is given in the right place to help you.

mniaal

a __ __ __ __ __

lanpt

__ __ __ n __

lear

__ e __ __

viling

l __ __ __ __ __

From school to home

Ask an adult at home to help you ...

1 Talk to someone at home about what you know of living and non-living things.

2 Now ask someone at home to help you complete the following questions:

a What did you like about this topic?

____

____

____

b What was hard to understand about this topic?

____

____

____

I understand. I understand a bit. I need more time to understand this.

3 **Look again at the checklist below. How are you doing now? Circle one face for each statement.**

- I can say if something is alive.
- I know the differences between living and non-living things.
- I can name some living and non-living things.

4 **Ask an adult at home to read and sign this.**

I have checked learning on this topic.

We have shared some understanding at home.

Signed: ______________________

Date: ______________

Teacher comment: ______________________________

____

Date: ______________

3.2 Living things around me

Living things live in different places

Plants and animals live in particular places. The same plants and animals do not live everywhere on Earth.

Plants and animals live in places where they can get the things they need.

Why don't you see many living things in the desert? Use the words in the box to help you say why.

shade cool water plants eat drink

You cannot see many living things in the desert because

____

____

____

____

Why can you see so many living things in the jungle? Use the words in the box to help you say why.

shade cool water plants eat drink

There are many living things in the jungle because

____

____

____

____

Check your science!

Looking for living things

**Work with someone at home.
Go outside and look for living things.**

Look at the picture. Where are good places to look for living things?

____

____

Why are living things found in these places?

____

____

Practising my science language

Making sentences

Try to say sentences using some of the science words from this topic:

light dark hot cold dry damp

For example: "Plants like to live in light places."

Write your sentences here:

In snowy places it is ______________________________________

______________________________________.

In a desert it is ______________________________________

______________________________________.

By a river it is ______________________________________

______________________________________.

From school to home

Ask an adult at home to help you ...

1. Talk to someone at home about what you know of living things around you.
2. Now ask someone at home to help you complete the following questions:

a What did you like about this topic?

____

____

____

b What was hard to understand about this topic?

____

____

____

I understand. I understand a bit. I need more time to understand this.

3 **Look again at the checklist below. How are you doing now? Circle one face for each statement.**

- I can say where some plants live.
- I can say where some animals live.

4 **Ask an adult at home to read and sign this.**

I have checked learning on this topic.

We have shared some understanding at home.

Signed: ______________________

Date: ______________

Teacher comment: ______________________________

____

Date: ______________

3.3 Eating to live

Eating a mix of foods is important

All living things need food to live.

There are different kinds of food. We should eat a mix of different foods to be healthy.

What can you say to the two children in the picture? Talk about it with someone at home. Tell them:

- **what foods are healthy**
- **what foods are less healthy**
- **what other foods they could eat.**

Write some of your ideas here:

Check your science!

Choosing foods

Compare Akim and Keira's shopping lists:

Akim's list	Keira's list
bananas	chocolate
cheese	milk
chicken	crisps
eggs	chicken
milk	bread
apples	pizza
onions	cake
tomatoes	sweets

Have Akim and Keira chosen a healthy mix of foods in their lists?

Think!

What can you take off the lists? What can you add?

Help Akim and Keira to buy the right mix of foods.

Cross out one thing on Keira's list to help her eat more healthily.

Choosing drinks

Fresh water is the most healthy drink. Why are some drinks not as healthy? Talk about this with an adult. Write some of your ideas here.

Practising my
science language

Food poem

Learn this poem. Practise saying it to people at home.

Rice is nice –

I could eat bread instead.

Meat is more than just a treat.

I think what I drink.

Names of fruit

Write the names of your three favourite fruits:

____

____

____

Missing words

Fill in the gaps with the right words. Choose from the box.

food groups   eat   healthy   drink

We ________________ water to stay alive. We ________________ fruit to stay ________________. Fruit and vegetables are one of the ________________ I learnt about.

From school to home

Ask an adult at home to help you ...

1. Talk to someone at home about why food and drink are important and why we should eat a mix of foods.
2. Now ask someone at home to help you complete the following questions:

a What did you like about this topic?

____

____

____

b What was hard to understand about this topic?

____

____

____

I understand. | I understand a bit. | I need more time to understand this.

3 **Look again at the checklist below. How are you doing now? Circle one face for each statement.**

- I can say where different foods come from.
- I can name healthy things to eat.
- I can say what is healthy to drink.

4 **Ask an adult at home to read and sign this.**

I have checked learning on this topic.

We have shared some understanding at home.

Signed: ______________________

Date: ______________

Teacher comment: ______________________________

____

Date: ______________

3.4 Baby animals

Babies grow into adults

All animals can have babies. Baby animals grow up to become adults.

When an animal becomes too old, it dies. Because the babies grow up into adults, they can take the place of the older ones that have died.

Look at the picture. Do you agree with the boy?

____

____

____

Check your science!

Same family

Look at the picture. Circle the animals that belong to the same family.

How do you know they are from this family?

What features do **only** the animals from the same family share?

Talk about it with someone at home.

Write three ideas here:

The features that this animal family shares are:

- ______________________________

  ____

- ______________________________

  ____

- ______________________________

  ____

Practising my

science language

Making words

How many science words about animals and babies can you make from these letters?

Try to make four to start with. Can you make more?

u b t a m p b y n i l h f l e s r o g

parent ________________ ________________

________________ ________________

________________ ________________

Understanding science words

Tell an adult what your words mean.

Do any of your words fit in the gaps below?

Write the correct words in the gaps.

Together, mum, dad, brother and sister make a ________________.

A person who has a child is a ________________.

A very young animal is called a ________________.

A chicken is an ________________, not a plant.

From school to home

Ask an adult at home to help you ...

1. Talk to someone at home about what you know of baby animals.
2. Now ask someone at home to help you complete the following questions:

a What did you like about this topic?

____

____

____

b What was hard to understand about this topic?

____

____

____

I understand.

I understand a bit.

I need more time to understand this.

3 **Look again at the checklist below. How are you doing now? Circle one face for each statement.**

- I can compare young animals with their parents.
- I know that families have groups called generations.

4 **Ask an adult at home to read and sign this.**

I have checked learning on this topic.

We have shared some understanding at home.

Signed: ______________________

Date: ______________

Teacher comment: ______________________________

____

Date: ______________

4 Pushes and pulls

4.1 Moving

There are many different types of movement

Things move in different ways. They might move fast or slowly. They might jump or swing. They might turn.

Look at the two animals. In what ways could they move? Write down some ideas.

____

____

____

How do other animals move?

____

____

____

Check your science!

Words for movement

Look at the pictures. Choose a word from the list to describe each movement.

slide turn crawl jump swing

Write the word under the picture. One has been done for you.

swing

____

____

____

____

____

Practising my

science language

Words and meanings

Draw lines to match the movements with their descriptions. One has been done for you.

jump	Slip along
slide	Move far in a short time
move fast	Move through the air
move slowly	Move up off the ground
spin	Move only a short distance in a long time
fly	Turn round and round

Sentences

How do you like to move? Do you like jumping? Do you like skipping? Make up two sentences about moving. Here is an example to help you.

I like jumping on a trampoline.

Write your two sentences below. Say the sentences to someone at home. Show them the movement in each sentence.

I like ______________________________

____

______________________________.

I like ______________________________

____

______________________________.

From school to home

Ask an adult at home to help you ...

1. Talk to someone at home about what you know of different types of movement.
2. Now ask someone at home to help you complete the following questions:

a What did you like about this topic?

____

____

____

b What was hard to understand about this topic?

____

____

____

I understand. | I understand a bit. | I need more time to understand this.

3 **Look again at the checklist below. How are you doing now? Circle one face for each statement.**

- I can spot different types of movement.
- I can name at least three different types of movement.

4 **Ask an adult at home to read and sign this.**

I have checked learning on this topic.

We have shared some understanding at home.

Signed: ______________________

Date: ______________

Teacher comment: ______________________________

____

Date: ______________

4.2 Different forces

Forces can make different things happen

A force can be a **push**, a **pull** or a **turning** force.

Forces can make things happen. They can cause things to start moving.

They can cause things that are moving to speed up, slow down or change direction.

Sometimes forces do not make things move.

Talk about what is happening in the picture with someone at home.

Write some of your ideas here:

Both teams are ______________________.

If 3 and 4 swap, I think ______________________.

If 1 and 6 swap, I think ______________________.

If 1 and 4 swap, I think ______________________.

Check your science!

Knowing which force to use

Look at the three pictures.

How can you make the objects move? What type of force is needed for each one?

Write the forces needed underneath the pictures.

______________________ ______________________ ______________________

Using more than one force

Look at this door. What forces do you use to open the door and close it again after you walk through?

Write your ideas here.

To open the door you have to ____________________ the door knob.

You have to ____________________ the door open to walk through.

When you close the door you use a ____________________ force.

What if the door opened the other way?

Would the forces you use change? Choose one answer and explain it.

No, the forces do not change because ____

____.

Yes, the forces change because ____

____.

Practising my
science language

Finding words about force

Below is a list of words from this topic.

Read all the words to someone at home.

Underline the words that are types of force.

push	move	faster	turn	pull	go

Using words about force

Pick two words from the list. Do something at home that uses each word.

For example: I made a ball roll **faster**.

Show someone at home. Write down what you did below.

1. ______________________________

____

____

____

2. ______________________________

____

____

____

From school to home

Ask an adult at home to help you ...

1. Talk to someone at home about what you know of pushing, pulling and turning forces and what they can do.

2. Now ask someone at home to help you complete the following questions:

a What did you like about this topic?

____

____

____

b What was hard to understand about this topic?

____

____

____

I understand. I understand a bit. I need more time to understand this.

3 **Look again at the checklist below. How are you doing now? Circle one face for each statement.**

- I can talk about different kinds of force.
- I can say what forces do.
- I know that pushes and pulls are kinds of force.

4 **Ask an adult at home to read and sign this.**

I have checked learning on this topic.

We have shared some understanding at home.

Signed: ______________________

Date: ______________

Teacher comment: ______________________________

____

Date: ______________

4.3 Speeding up and slowing down

Forces can change how things move

We can use a force to make moving things go faster or slower. We can also use a force to make moving things change direction.

Talk about the children's ideas with someone at home.

What do you think about each one? Write some of your ideas here:

"I think the ball will go down the hill and keep going."

I agree / I agree a little bit / I disagree because ____________________

____

____.

"I think the ball will get faster as it goes down."

I agree / I agree a little bit / I disagree because ____________________

____

____.

"I think the ball will move but will slow down again at the bottom."

I agree / I agree a little bit / I disagree because ____________________

____

____.

Check your science!

Describing what will happen

Look at the picture of the toy car at the top of the ramp.

What will happen to the car when Akim lets go?

Choose the right sentence for each place to describe what is happening.

Write the number in the box for each place.

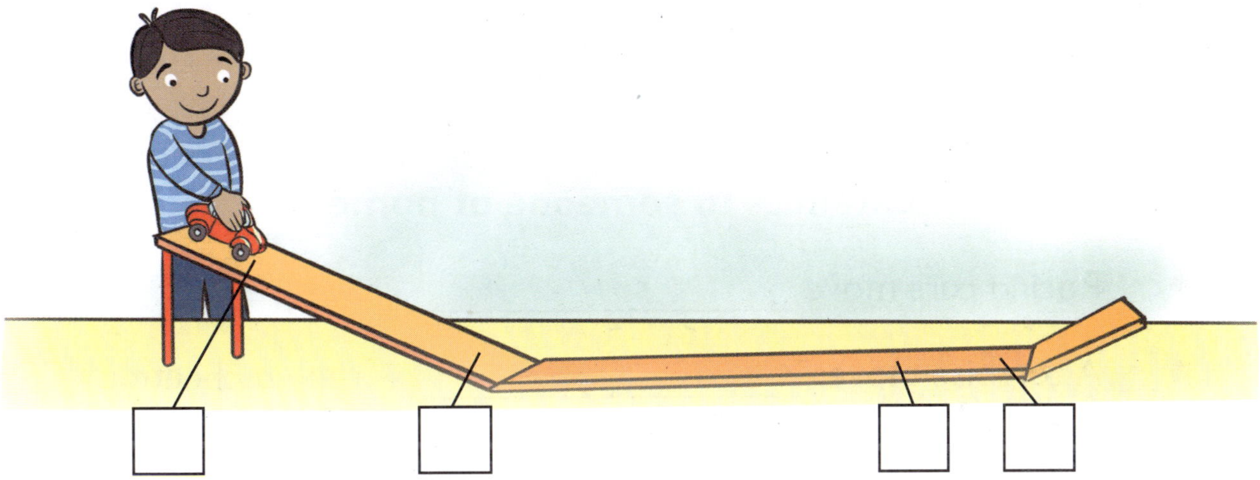

1. The car slows down.
2. The car starts moving.
3. The car stops.
4. The car is moving fast.

Predicting and testing

How can you make the toy car go more slowly on the ramp?

If you have a car or a ball, try your idea at home.

What did you find out? Write about it here.

____

____

____

Practising my

science language

Putting words in order

Arrange these words from fast to slow.

slower stop fast

Write the words below.

________________ ________________ ________________

Sentences

Use words from the list above to finish these sentences. Then say the sentences to someone at home.

- Racing cars move ________________.
- A tortoise moves ________________ than a cheetah.
- A bus should ________________ before passengers can get on.
- A hippo can sometimes move ________________.

From school to home

Ask an adult at home to help you ...

1. Talk to someone at home about what you know of speeding up and slowing down.
2. Now ask someone at home to help you complete the following questions:

a What did you like about this topic?

____

____

____

b What was hard to understand about this topic?

____

____

____

I understand.

I understand a bit.

I need more time to understand this.

3 **Look again at the checklist below. How are you doing now? Circle one face for each statement.**

- I can see changes in movement.
- I can compare speeding up and slowing down.
- I can talk about what makes movement change.

4 **Ask an adult at home to read and sign this.**

I have checked learning on this topic.

We have shared some understanding at home.

Signed: ____________________

Date: ____________

Teacher comment: __________________________

____

Date: ____________

5 Making sounds

5.1 Where does sound come from?

Actions can make sounds

You can make sounds by doing an action with an object. Some objects make a sound when you shake them.

How can you make sounds with the other objects? Write some of your ideas below.

Object	How I can make a sound with it
	I can
	I can
	I can

Check your science!

Sounds from objects

Practise making and listening to sounds made with mystery objects. Ask someone at home to do it with you.

Close your eyes. The other person makes a sound using an object from around your house. Now swap around.

Draw some of the objects you used. Put a tick next to the ones you could name just from listening.

Sounds outside

Go outside during the day. Stand quietly and listen. What animals can you hear?

____

What other sounds can you hear?

____

Go outside at night. Stand quietly and listen. What animals can you hear?

____

What sounds can you hear at night but not during the day?

____

Practising my

science language

Making sentences

Choose three of the words from this topic to make sentences.

Here are some words you can choose from:

sound	voice	hear	bang	hit	drum	animal	listen

For example: "I can hear a bird outside."

Say the sentences to someone at home.

Quiz time!

Below is a quiz about sound. Write your answers. Ask someone at home. Write their answers.

1. What is your favourite sound?

   Your answer: ______________________ Their answer: ______________________

2. What animal sound did you hear today?

   Your answer: ______________________ Their answer: ______________________

3. What makes a sound in the kitchen?

   Your answer: ______________________ Their answer: ______________________

From school to home

Ask an adult at home to help you ...

1. Talk to someone at home about where sounds come from.
2. Now ask someone at home to help you complete the following questions:

a What did you like about this topic?

____

____

____

b What was hard to understand about this topic?

____

____

____

I understand.

I understand a bit.

I need more time to understand this.

3 **Look again at the checklist below. How are you doing now? Circle one face for each statement.**

- I can say where sounds come from.
- I can tell different sounds apart.
- I can use words to say what different sounds are like.

4 **Ask an adult at home to read and sign this.**

I have checked learning on this topic.

We have shared some understanding at home.

Signed: ______________________

Date: ______________

Teacher comment: ____________________________

____

Date: ______________

5.2 Loud and soft

Sounds far away are hard to hear

Sounds can be loud or soft. Loud sounds are easy to hear. Soft sounds are harder to hear.

It is harder to hear sounds when they are far away than when they are close.

Alena is playing the guitar but Malik cannot hear anything. He thinks there might be something wrong with the guitar.

Do you think Malik is right?
Circle your answer: **I think Malik is right / is not right.**

What other reasons could there be? Here are some clues:

- **Is Malik close to the guitar or far away?**
- **Is Alena playing loudly?**

Talk about your ideas with someone at home. Write some of your ideas here.

I think that Malik ______________________________

____

I think that Alena ______________________________

____

Check your science!

Understanding loud and soft

This bell rings in a school when it is playtime. It is important that everyone can hear it.

How can we make sure that everyone hears the bell? These children have some ideas.

Tick the ones that you think will work.

Practising my

science language

Word meanings

Draw lines to match the words to their descriptions. One has been done for you.

soft	A gentle, quiet sound
loud	Something you hear with your ears
sound	Talking very quietly
whisper	A long way away
far	A big sound

How loud?

Put these things in order of how loud they are. Write numbers from 1 to 4 in the boxes. Write "1"for the loudest sound and "4" for the softest sound.

Then match each sound to the right key word. Choose words from the box. Write the words in the spaces.

Key words:

loud soft loudest softest

Waves on the beach ☐ ____________________

Dripping tap ☐ ____________________

Rainstorm ☐ ____________________

Running a bath ☐ ____________________

From school to home

Ask an adult at home to help you ...

1. Talk to someone at home about what you know of loud and soft sounds.

2. Now ask someone at home to help you complete the following questions:

a What did you like about this topic?

___

___

___

b What was hard to understand about this topic?

___

___

___

I understand. I understand a bit. I need more time to understand this.

3 **Look again at the checklist below. How are you doing now? Circle one face for each statement.**

- I know the difference between loud and soft sounds.
- I can describe some soft sounds and some loud sounds.
- I know how to make loud and soft sounds.
- I can say what happens to a sound when I move towards or away from it.

4 **Ask an adult at home to read and sign this.**

I have checked learning on this topic.

We have shared some understanding at home.

Signed: ______________________

Date: ______________

Teacher comment: ______________________________

____

Date: ______________

5.3 Protecting my hearing

We protect our ears so they can hear sound

Your ears can help to tell you what is going on around you. The siren from a police car warns you that there is an emergency. When you hear the car coming, you can make sure that you are not in the way.

Very loud sounds can damage your ears. You can protect your ears with ear defenders.

Where would it be good to wear ear defenders? Write some ideas here:

____

____

____

Check your science!

Choosing and testing ideas

Malik cannot sleep. A dog keeps barking during the night. Amanda has some ideas:

- Make some ear plugs.
- Make sure the windows are closed.
- Draw the curtains.

Which of Amanda's ideas is best?

The best idea is to ____.

Explain why you think it is the best idea.

I think it is the best idea because ______________________________

____.

Amanda and Malik are trying to find which material is best for ear plugs.

Help Amanda and Malik to test the materials.

How could they test the two materials? Write your ideas here.

____

____

____

____

Practising my

science language

Mixed-up words

Arrange the letters to make science words from this topic. One has been done for you.

o u d l l o u d

o s n d u _ _ _ n _

o e r t p c t _ r _ _ _ _ _

a r e s e _ _ _

Using science words

Use the words you have found in sentences.

Write three sentences to explain what the science words mean.

For example: "A big noise is loud."

1. ______________________________

____

____

2. ______________________________

____

____

3. ______________________________

____

____

Say the sentences to someone at home.

From school to home

Ask an adult at home to help you ...

1. Talk to someone at home about protecting your hearing against damaging sounds.
2. Now ask someone at home to help you complete the following questions:

a What did you like about this topic?

____

____

____

b What was hard to understand about this topic?

____

____

____

I understand. I understand a bit. I need more time to understand this.

3 **Look again at the checklist below. How are you doing now? Circle one face for each statement.**

- I know that we hear sound when it enters our ears.
- I can say what can damage my hearing.
- I can say how to protect my hearing.
- I can say how hearing can help keep me safe.

4 **Ask an adult at home to read and sign this.**

I have checked learning on this topic.

We have shared some understanding at home.

Signed: ____________________

Date: ______________

Teacher comment: ______________________________

____

Date: ______________

6 Growing plants

6.1 Parts of a plant

Plants are alive

There are many different kinds of plant. Trees, shrubs and grasses are all types of plant.

Plants have a stem, leaves and roots. Some plants have flowers. Plants are living things.

How do you know that the tree is alive? ______________________

____

____

What other signs might you see to tell you that the tree is alive? Write one thing.

____

____

Check your science!

Labelling a plant

Look at the plant. Label the parts in the boxes.

Add a label to the picture to show where you would look for the roots.

Draw and label a plant you have at home.

Practising my

science language

Finding words

Look at the word puzzle. Use the clues to find science words from this topic.

Circle the word in the puzzle and write it next to the clue.

The first one has been done for you.

a	p	b	c	s	t	d	x	y	l	h
v	l	t	u	t	k	m	f	g	i	e
d	a	f	f	e	r	e	l	t	v	c
f	n	r	a	m	e	v	o	k	i	q
n	t	o	f	a	b	a	w	e	n	g
r	x	l	e	a	f	l	e	e	g	p
t	m	o	v	e	p	a	r	o	o	t
i	j	r	u	x	g	r	o	w	s	g
p	a	d	w	e	d	z	d	h	i	t

Clues:

All living things can do this. m o v e

A living thing with leaves: p _ _ _ _

When a living thing gets bigger, it _ r _ _ _.

The part of the plant that holds the leaves up: _ _ _ m

Which other words from the topic can you find? Write them here:

____

____

From school to home

Ask an adult at home to help you ...

1. **Talk to someone at home about plants and their parts.**
2. **Now ask someone at home to help you complete the following questions:**

a What did you like about this topic?

____

____

____

b What was hard to understand about this topic?

____

____

____

I understand. I understand a bit. I need more time to understand this.

3 **Look again at the checklist below. How are you doing now? Circle one face for each statement.**

- I can name the parts of a plant.
- I know about different types of plant.

4 **Ask an adult at home to read and sign this.**

I have checked learning on this topic.

We have shared some understanding at home.

Signed: ______________________

Date: ______________

Teacher comment: ______________________________

____

Date: ______________

6.2 Where do plants come from?

Seeds need things to grow

Adult plants make seeds. Seeds grow into new plants.

Seeds need things before they can start to grow.

Will any of the seeds grow? Will they all grow? Put a tick next to any pot of seeds in the picture that you think will grow.

Explain your choice.

____

____

____

Check your science!

Testing an idea

Ask someone at home to get some seeds. You are going to do a test to see if they need soil to grow.

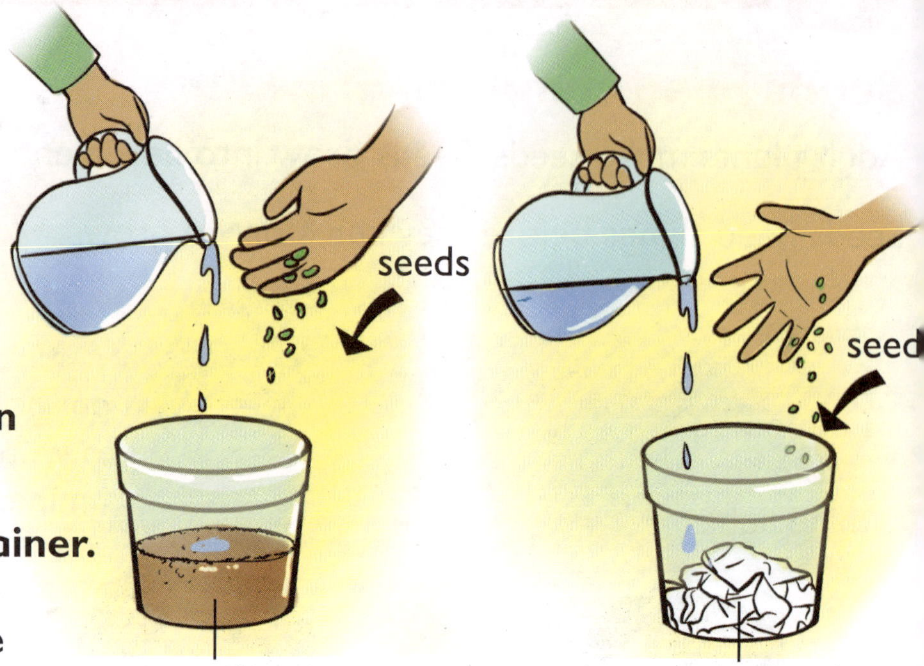

You will need two small containers. Put soil in one and a paper towel in the other.

Add seeds to each container. Water both so that the soil and paper towel are just wet.

Put the two containers in the same place. Water the seeds every day so that the soil and paper towel do not dry out.

Look at the seeds every day.

Write what happens to the seeds here:

The seeds with soil ______________________________

____

____

The seeds with paper towel ______________________________

____

____

Do seeds need soil to grow? Tick the right box. Yes ☐ No ☐

Practising my

science language

Reading out loud

Say these questions to someone at home. They must answer "yes" or "no".

- Can tests help us find out what seeds need? **Yes** or **no**
- Do seeds need water to grow? **Yes** or **no**
- Do seeds need light to start growing? **Yes** or **no**
- Do adult plants make seeds? **Yes** or **no**
- Can grass grow into a tree? **Yes** or **no**
- Do seeds grow into adult plants? **Yes** or **no**

Sentences

What else have you learnt in this topic?

Make up two sentences of your own.

Say them out loud. Write them here.

1. I have learnt that ____

   ____.

2. I have learnt that ____

   ____.

Make a poster

Make a poster to tell people about plants or growing seeds.

Use some of your science words from this topic.

Add a colourful picture to your poster.

From school to home

Ask an adult at home to help you ...

1. Talk to someone at home about where plants come from and what seeds need to grow.
2. Now ask someone at home to help you complete the following questions:

a What did you like about this topic?

____

____

____

b What was hard to understand about this topic?

____

____

____

I understand.

I understand a bit.

I need more time to understand this.

3 **Look again at the checklist below. How are you doing now? Circle one face for each statement.**

- I know that seeds grow into new plants.
- I can predict why seeds grow.
- I know that seeds need water to start growing.

4 **Ask an adult at home to read and sign this.**

I have checked learning on this topic.

We have shared some understanding at home.

Signed: ______________________

Date: ______________

Teacher comment: ______________________________

____

Date: ______________

6.3 What plants need

Plants need water and light

Plants are living things. They need things like light and water to live and grow.

Where can plants in the desert get their water? Write what you think here.

They could get their water from ______________________________

____

____

____

What happens to a plant if it does not get enough water? Write what you think here.

If a plant does not get enough water it ______________________

____

____

____

Check your science!

Fair tests

We can do tests to find out what plants need. We need to make our test fair.

These two children are trying to find out if plants need light to grow.

They want to be sure that only light or dark causes differences.

How can they make the test fair? Tick the correct sentences: ✔

- Both plants should be put in the light. ☐
- Only one plant should be put in the light. ☐
- Only one plant should be watered. ☐
- Both plants should have the same amount of water. ☐
- The plants should be the same. ☐

Practising my

science language

Missing words

Use words from the box to fill in the gaps in the sentences.

desert	fair	living	need

- Plants ____________________ water to grow.
- Even in the ____________________ there is some water.
- To find out if plants need something we can do a ____________________ test.
- A plant is a ____________________ thing.

A growing poem

Fill in the words of this poem. Learn it and share it with someone at home.

Choose words from the box:

grow	Water	plant	leaves

Sunshine makes the plants ____________________ high.

____________________ falls down from the sky.

When the ____________________ gets both of these,

It will smile and wave its ____________________.

From school to home

Ask an adult at home to help you ...

1. Talk to someone at home about the importance of water and light for plants and what it means to do a fair test.

2. Now ask someone at home to help you complete the following questions:

a What did you like about this topic?

____

____

____

b What was hard to understand about this topic?

____

____

____

I understand.

I understand a bit.

I need more time to understand this.

3 **Look again at the checklist below. How are you doing now? Circle one face for each statement.**

- I know that plants need water to live and grow.
- I know that plants need light to live and grow.
- I can do a fair test.

4 **Ask an adult at home to read and sign this.**

I have checked learning on this topic.

We have shared some understanding at home.

Signed: ______________________

Date: _____________

Teacher comment: ____________________________

____

Date: _____________